EUROPE

Alexis Roumanis

LET'S READ
AV2
BY WEIGL™
ADDED VALUE • AUDIO VISUAL

www.av2books.com

LET'S READ
AV²
BY WEIGL™
ADDED VALUE • AUDIO VISUAL

Go to **www.av2books.com**, and enter this book's unique code.

BOOK CODE

W394736

AV² **by Weigl** brings you media enhanced books that support active learning.

AV² provides enriched content that supplements and complements this book. Weigl's AV² books strive to create inspired learning and engage young minds in a total learning experience.

Your AV² Media Enhanced books come alive with...

Audio
Listen to sections of the book read aloud.

Video
Watch informative video clips.

Embedded Weblinks
Gain additional information for research.

Key Words
Study vocabulary, and complete a matching word activity.

Quizzes
Test your knowledge.

Slide Show
View images and captions, and prepare a presentation.

Try This!
Complete activities and hands-on experiments.

... and much, much more!

Published by AV² by Weigl
350 5th Avenue, 59th Floor New York, NY 10118
Websites: www.av2books.com   www.weigl.com

Library of Congress Cataloging-in-Publication Data

Roumanis, Alexis.
 Europe / Alexis Roumanis.
     pages cm. -- (Exploring continents)
 Includes bibliographical references and index.
 ISBN 978-1-4896-3038-4 (hard cover : alk. paper) -- ISBN 978-1-4896-3039-1 (soft cover : alk. paper) --
 ISBN 978-1-4896-3040-7 (single user ebook) -- ISBN 978-1-4896-3041-4 (multi-user ebook)
 1. Europe--Juvenile literature. I. Title.
 D1051.R68 2014
 940--dc23
                                    2014044126

Printed in the United States of America in Brainerd, Minnesota
1 2 3 4 5 6 7 8 9 0 18 17 16 15 14

122014   Project Coordinator: Jared Siemens
WEP051214   Design: Mandy Christiansen

Weigl acknowledges iStock and Getty Images as the primary image suppliers for this title.

EUROPE

Contents

2 AV² Book Code
4 Get to Know Europe
6 Where Is Europe?
8 Looking at the Land
10 The Animals of Europe
12 European Plants
14 Europe's History
16 People in Europe
18 Europe Today
20 Only in Europe
22 Europe Quiz
24 Key Words/Log on to
    www.av2books.com

Welcome to Europe.
It is the second smallest continent.

This is the
shape of Europe.
Asia lies to the
east of Europe.
Africa sits to the south.

Where Is Europe?

Arctic Ocean

Arctic Ocean

North America

EUROPE

Asia

Pacific Ocean

Atlantic Ocean

Africa

Pacific Ocean

South America

Indian Ocean

Australia

N

W   E

S

Antarctica

Two oceans touch
the coast of Europe.

Europe is made up of many different landforms. Deserts, glaciers, mountains, plains, and rainforests can all be found in Europe.

The Highlands of Iceland are the biggest desert in Europe.

Great Britain is Europe's largest island.

Lake Ladoga is the largest lake in Europe.

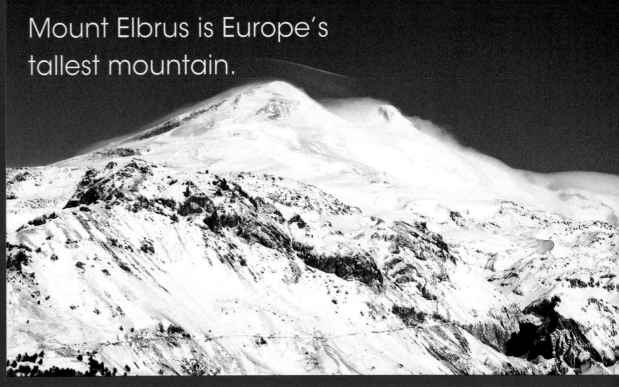

Mount Elbrus is Europe's tallest mountain.

The Volga River is the longest river in Europe.

Puffins flap their wings to swim under water.

The European brown hare is the fastest land animal in Europe.

The European bison is the largest land animal in Europe.

Europe is home to some of the world's most unique animals. Many different kinds of animals live there.

The red fox uses its tail like a scarf to keep its face warm.

There are only about 300 Iberian lynx left in the world.

Europe is home to many different types of plants.

Spain grows more olives than any other country in the world.

Pear trees first came from Europe.

A yew tree in England is the oldest living tree in Europe. It is more than 4,000 years old.

A chestnut tree in Sicily is the widest tree in the world.

Juniper berries are sometimes used to flavor food.

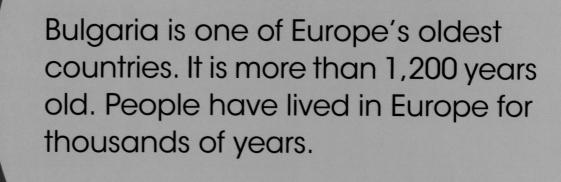

Bulgaria is one of Europe's oldest countries. It is more than 1,200 years old. People have lived in Europe for thousands of years.

The Sámi are one of the first peoples of Europe.

Many kinds of people live in Europe. Each group of people is special in its own way.

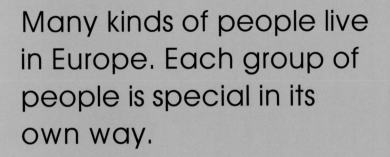

Some Russian women wear a hat called a kokoshnik on their heads.

Wooden shoes help some Dutch farmers walk on muddy soil.

More than 742 million people live in Europe. Russia has more land than any other country in Europe.

Moscow, Russia has more people than any other city in Europe.

There are many things that can be found only in Europe.
People come from all over the world to visit this continent.

Thousands of people visit the Acropolis in Athens every day.

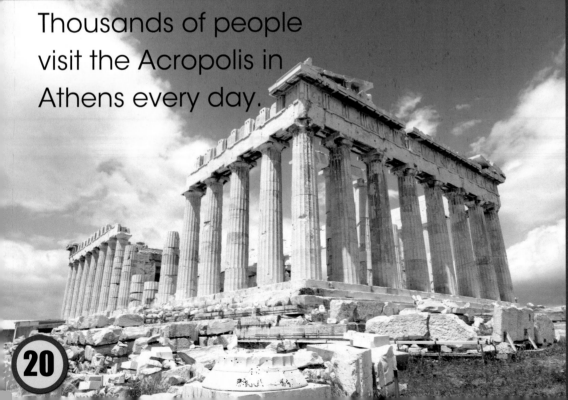

The Louvre Museum in Paris has more visitors each year than any other art museum in the world.

The Colosseum is an ancient arena in Rome.

The steep fjords of Norway are best viewed by boat.

Stonehenge in England is more than 5,000 years old.

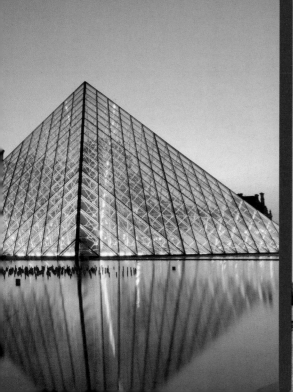

Europe Quiz

See what you have learned about the continent of Europe.

What do these pictures tell you about Europe?

23

KEY WORDS

Research has shown that as much as 65 percent of all written material published in English is made up of 300 words. These 300 words cannot be taught using pictures or learned by sounding them out. They must be recognized by sight. This book contains 80 common sight words to help young readers improve their reading fluency and comprehension. This book also teaches young readers several important content words, such as proper nouns. These words are paired with pictures to aid in learning and improve understanding.

Page	Sight Words First Appearance
4	is, it, second, the, to
7	of, this, two, where
8	all, and, are, be, can, different, found, great, in, made, many, most, mountains, up
9	river
10	animal, land, their, under, water
11	a, about, face, home, its, keep, kinds, left, like, live, most, only, some, there, uses, world
12	any, came, country, first, from, grows, more, old, other, plants, than, tree, years
13	food, sometimes
15	for, have, one, people
16	each, group, help, on, own
17	men
19	city, has
20	an, come, day, every, over, that, things
21	by

Page	Content Words First Appearance
4	continent, Europe
7	Africa, Asia, coast, oceans, shape
8	desert, glaciers, Great Britain, Iceland, lake, landforms, plains, rainforests
10	bison, hare, puffins
11	fox, lynx, scarf
12	England, olives, pear, Spain, yew
13	berries, chestnut, flavor, Sicily
15	Bulgaria
16	farmers, hat, shoes
17	dancers, dresses, Scotland, skirts
19	Russia, London
20	arena, museum, Athens, Paris, Rome
21	boat, Norway

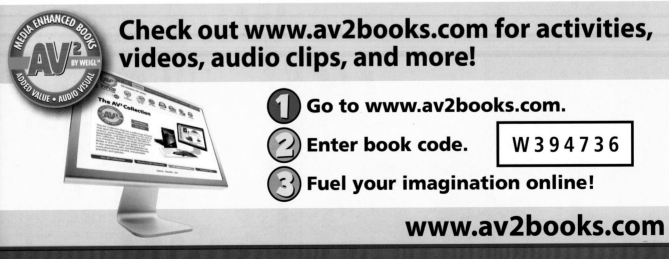